Social Media Marketing

Learn The Social Media Influence And Witness The Power Of Social Media For Business

William Chang

Table of Contents

Introduction

In a world where the only permanent thing is change, it is but natural to adapt to these new and high-tech ways of delivering messages all over the planet. We currently live in a modern and fast paced society. Nowadays, people have the power to connect to their friends and loved ones with just one click of a button. Hence, many opportunities are now available through the Internet. People are now putting their businesses online, whether small, medium-sized or simply trying to break into the market. They want to make sure that they will be seen, felt and be able to attract people in this modern society.

In this regard, I thank you and congratulate you for purchasing this book about *Social Media Marketing*. You now have a copy of this valuable book that will show you the tricks of the trade of social media marketing and will provide you with tips and guidelines on how to utilize social media effectively.

This book will show you best social media strategies that will help you improve your branding and attract people on all social media sites every single day. You will be provided with an overview of each popular social media site and how they work; basic tools of social media marketing and so much more. So what are you waiting for? Go ahead and explore the limitless possibilities and the power of social media marketing.

Happy reading!

Chapter 1 - Why is Social Media Marketing Important?

Social media marketing is one of the methods used to gain attention in marketing through social media sites. It uses these sites to promote businesses, products and services – in short advertisements. Using the social feature of the web, social media marketing enables every individual to connect and intermingle in a dynamic and personal way as opposed to the traditional way of marketing.

This type of marketing usually centers its efforts on creating content that will attract attention and encourage readers to share it with their own social network. When an individual starts to share a certain topic; may it be a blog, a product or service – this can spread from user to user and will continue to resonate all over the net, assuming that it became popular. This viral potential has an enormous number of publicity benefits.

So far, this has been a widely popular method in marketing products and services because of its convenience, faster response time and popularity. Social media marketing caters a wide array of people. Anyone, as in ANYONE can use this method. For personal use, business use, organizations, small to medium sized businesses; even those large and well-known businesses use this kind of marketing. As long as you are internet savvy and knowledgeable in various social media sites, you can utilize and start using this avenue.

However, it's not that simple. You can't just log in or make your own page and start promoting whatever products or service you represent. You must remember that there are many things that must be considered. Content for one, obviously plays a crucial role in having a successful outcome. Timing and strategy should also be considered. Social media marketing can either make or break you. Most people think that because of the promise of high rewards and irresistible success, it's easy to just jump right in. If you are not using it effectively and well enough to your advantage, this can be the biggest waste of time that you will ever make for your business. Make sure that you know how to do it right and you are equipped with the necessary know-hows to avoid failure and disappointment on your side.

Why should you do it?

Because social media sites are continuously becoming popular, this is the best avenue to share and discover new content. It feeds on unearthing new and exciting content, stories and other useful things that people may need in their life. This can also build links or associations that will someday be useful for you. Best of all it's free. You start small and for all you know, you are already reaching out to millions and millions of people. Remember, most people, businesses or brands start small through simple posting of videos, blogs, or having to set up pages on social media sites. As long as you build your brand, gain trust and remain unique, you will go a long way.

To further provide you with more ideas regarding social media, here are some of the most popular social media marketing sites that you can visit. I know that you are familiar with most of these sites – heck, you may even have accounts on every one:

- Facebook
- Instagram
- Twitter
- Pinterest
- Google +
- LinkedIn
- YouTube

So what are you waiting for? There's nothing to lose if you try delving into the social media marketing world. Remember that the longer you delay, the more you are losing out on. If social media marketing is done right, this will lead to better profitability and success that you are aiming for.

Chapter 2 - What Power Lies In Online Marketing To Make Money?

As an online entrepreneur and seller, I believe that there are some factors that make online marketing a great way to make money. As we all are aware, a lot of people in the world (yes, globally) are connected with the Internet, particularly by social media. Since it has been like a community where people get to meet and greet each other, it's no wonder why business have also been involved in it.

Though earning is our main purpose in online marketing, there are some things that we need to consider and give attention to.

I want to give you some of the tips and advice on how can you effectively earn money from online marketing.

- **Be Willing.** It takes motivation and willingness for you to succeed in this kind of business, so you better be ready and stay positive!
- **Research.** Know and learn everything you have to, from accessing an Internet connection to the making of accounts, tallying your products, computing your capital etc. Be knowledgeable enough before you push through.
- **Be Physically Ready.** This has been a struggle for me since I have no assistant when I buy my products from my supplier, especially when there are lots of orders to pick up and staying up for long hours in front of the computer or your mobile phone answering inquiries can be very tiring too, so you better be physically healthy and try to eat clean.
- **Be Patient.** You will encounter different customers of different characteristics, so be patient and know how to deal "kindly" with them.

How Can It Help You Earn?

Selling online can help you earn by, first, promoting your business, whether it is a website, a Facebook page, an instagram online shop or whatever. You must take time to promote of course so that people will get to know you and for you to gain customers. Once trust is developed between you and your customers, you can assure a fast earning. Lastly, do not spend a lot from your earnings. It is okay to reward yourself, but be sure that you are not consuming everything to the point that you do not have enough money to sustain the business. Spend wisely.

Can Anyone Do It?

In my personal opinion, not everybody can do it. Only people with much perseverance, diligence and patience will be able to succeed in this kind of marketing. Don't worry, everybody feels nervous at first, but remember, "a quitter never wins and a winner never quits!" You MUST be persistent.

How Sure Is It?

You can be assured 100% that you are going to earn from it if you have learned how to handle the money that's coming in and out of your business. You will only spend the profit, and not the capital. Be sure not to give too many discounts that may cause you to earn significantly less money. Be consistent, be wise and be careful of scammers and bogus buyers.

Chapter 3 - What Can You Get With Social Media Marketing?

Today we can say that Social Media Marketing or SMM for short is the most common marketing tool that almost all businesses use. But what is Social Media Marketing in the first place? This is the process where the website traffic is gained by seeking attention through social media sites. Their goal is to create content that will help the company better expose their brand and reach more customers. It's much easier and efficient to know about people looking for particular products or services, allowing you to improve marketing efforts to make the business grow. These are the benefits from using Social Media Marketing. Of course, for you to reap the rewards, you should be consistent in everything you do and that's when your hard work will pay off.

1. **Your brand will be known.** Through social media your brand has the potential to be known worldwide. It is the fastest and most cost-effective way to broadcast your business compared to print or even television because it does the job for you. With this, you will be able to reach new customers and existing customers will be more familiar with your brand and this will make it very recognizable. Repetitive exposure will entice consumers to buy certain products. To start with, you can create a name that is unique. You could also design a logo that is slick and make a slogan which is catchy. Your brand will be exposed to a large number of consumers, be it local, nationwide or even global. This will affect their behavior and preferences when shopping. You will have a large audience to 'like 'or 'follow' your updates and business if they choose to. This will also enable customer interactions using the same kind of products or business wherein they could exchange ideas. Before you know it, they are already the brand-builders of the products or services you are offering. With that, search engine rankings will be less important.

2. **Your brand will be legitimized.** Any business, of course, would like to have legitimate products or services. Now that a lot of customers are using your product or service, you can say that it's legitimized. You will be able to showcase your business and have a good reputation. When you have a good reputation, customers will inquire about your name and the products or

services that you offer. They want to know what the company is all about and what the product is for. With that in mind, you will make skeptical consumers into customers. Different customers from all walks of life will be aware of the products or services you are selling. In this case, customers will not worry about the quality of your products or services, even if they use it over and over again because they find you and your brand highly credible. Your page should always be updated with comments, new posts or reviews for consumers to know that your brand is still active and being used by many. Keeping a good interactive customer relationship will help you immensely. This is one of the best parts of social media marketing, it makes it very simple to personally interact with customers all over the world in no time at all.

3. **Your sales will increase.** We are very particular about the return on investment or ROI. If a lot of people are viewing the products or services you are selling, there's a higher chance that you will make sales. Reaching a large market online will result in a higher conversion rate. But you also need to interact with other people and build a good relationship for them to buy from you. A lot of customers want to do business with PEOPLE not with COMPANIES (always keep this in mind. Never hide behind the mask of a company), so you should personally attend to their queries. Great promotions like giving special discounts or prizes are a big help for the business to earn more sales. Also, by getting in touch with your customers and keeping them informed about the latest updates regarding your business, you will generate revenue as well. Another way is putting content, like pictures or videos, about how the products work so you will have an idea before you buy or use such services. Comments and reviews will be a plus, making consumers decide that they are getting the best bang for their buck. The more they know about you and your business, the higher the revenue will be. Transparency is vital!

4. **Your service will improve.** Knowing your customers' wants and needs will be a big factor when determining what to offer them and how to improve your service. This will help you know your audience better. Thus, it will give you more leads and that means more customers who will spread the word about you and

your business. They will give you reviews or feedback (either positive or negative) about the product or business, which in turn you must acknowledge. From there, you can take the next step on how to improve your service and make it better. Because as soon as customers try and test your brand, and prove that everything you advertise is true, they will be your loyal customers telling everybody the good things about your product as well as the excellent customer service they experienced with you. So the next time new or existing customers stumble upon your product, they will buy it without even thinking twice. It is very important for any kind of business to keep excellent communication between you and your customers. Making happy and satisfied customers will keep you in business for a long time. After all, customers are always right (usually).

5. **You can share your knowledge.** For every product you sell, you explain how it works and what benefits customers are getting from it. Aside from that you're able to share with them things that they do not know yet. Getting ideas is one of the best parts of social networks. Customers get ideas from you and vice versa. You can also educate your customers by sharing your knowledge and experience by writing an article, blogging or putting up videos to let them know about your expertise.

Chapter 4 - The Basics Of Social Media Marketing

Social Media Marketing is now regarded as the most powerful tool to foster real-time and responsive engagement with people – regardless of the location, demographics, and interests. Let's be quite frank, shall we? All you want is to conquer the digital world with your branding and business. Without the likes and the efficacy of Social Media to date, you would probably end up distributing reams and reams of flyers every day to promote your business.

The 'magic' of Social Media Marketing is here so we can make use of it, manipulate it, learn from, benefit from it and eventually master it. It will not inundate you with immediate revenue, but it will provide you with all the instruments you need for building long-term business relationships, finding resources, and strengthening your branding strategies. All of these, in return, will make way for big results in the long run.

To truly benefit from Social Media Marketing, it is a MUST to understand its fundamentals. These are the basic principles that you need to bear in mind all throughout the process of creating your niche brand on the Web.

1. **You should listen.** As a businessperson, you should understand what other people need and want. Take the time to 'listen' to their woes, concerns, dreams and plans by reading what they have to say online. Listening is a crucial part of understanding your target audience as a whole. The most successful product developers are those capable of accessing the right information about their customer's needs. Use all the data you can get in choosing the right platform to use for your online marketing. Listening to your competitors is just as crucial. A strong branding strategy also requires outsmarting the other key players.

   These are the other things that you should also listen to:

   • Listen to the trends and the fads that your chosen demographics often try;

   • Listen to the 'changing' Internet habits of your target customers;

   • Listen to the latest developments in the world of applications and other social media management tools

2. **You should focus**. You can't work like Santa Clause all the time. You are not there to grant the diverse wishes of all the people online. Learn to focus on the specifics. Focusing on a core strategy for your marketing is vital. Creating well-written and optimized content will eventually give you better results than dabbling all the time. To be more specific, you should take note of the following:

   - Focus on a specific niche while understanding the sub-niches it may have;

   - Focus on one or two platforms at a time; social media marketing is not about who can juggle better. Rather, it focuses on who responds better.

   - Focus on the use of another supplemental affiliate marketing tool that is highly compatible with social media you aim to use.

3. **You should offer quality**. Quality should be the primary goal. You could gain better results if you are able to capture a 'quality' audience who is eager to keep your brand afloat on the Web. Note that you could instantly have hundreds of thousands of 'LIKERS' AND 'FOLLOWERS', but they may not necessarily be willing to take further actions than clicking the like or follow button. Quality products and branding strategies are all essential components of a successful overall marketing strategy.

   Working with and for quality service and products is tantamount to eliminating the need for future crisis management.

4. **You should be patient.** You cannot make it rain instantly. It takes time. It takes patience. Similar principles should also be applied to social media marketing. For example, traffic may start kicking in when you have already made quite a few attempts to linking your sites or when you have created or obtained strong keywords for your search engine optimization. Remember that time is crucial and vital when finding the best online marketing strategy for your business.

   Mastering the tools and the art of social media marketing also requires a great deal of patience. It is not exactly something that you can make automatic. You need patience and learn and understand the tools. You will also use your patience in reviewing and questioning them.

5. **You should be compound**. You need to understand that the result of one strategy may lead to the utilization of other strategies. Thus, making your own social media marketing tools compound. To illustrate an example, well-written web content may go viral on different social media platforms in no time. This will then allow your web content to be searched several times using Google, Bing, and the like, which will also eventually offer you opportunities to improve your visibility.

   In order to gain compound means of marketing, you can also check some free tools that are just as efficient. For example, the use of Google Analytics and Google Web tools can be utilized as a supplement for creating top-notch Web content that succeeds on useful keywords.

6. **You should influence.** It is safe to say that you cannot achieve the best results alone- no matter how excellent the content and articles are. The world of social media marketing also entails the use of 'influence' in broadening your chances to be seen and to be wanted. Spy if you must, if this is deemed the best method of knowing the correct 'digital network' to work with. Working collaboratively with other website owners sometimes produces a surprising outcome as well.

7. **You should have values**. It is a false belief that the use of social media marketing strategies is to solely promote your products. That is the basic principle, but there should be more than that. The added value you offer to your potential clients and Internet users will make your products even more enticing. Providing added value to your products will also produce amazing results in the long-run.

8. **You should acknowledge**. Never shun negative comments. Treat them just as relevant as the positive feedback you receive from your clients. Keep in mind that any form of feedback is essential to improving your products and your strategies as well. Acknowledging all comments you obtain from various social media platforms will also send a positive message about your responsiveness and professionalism.

   Information can be spread at light speed through social media. For businesspeople that are rather passive, a negative comment about the product can be immediately circulated on the Web in no time.

This is another reason why acknowledging or responding to what people say on the web professionally is essential.

9. **You should be accessible.** What's the point of using a 'social' platform if you are not available to socialize? One of the major pet peeves of clients is the inability of the business owners to respond or at least interact with their customers. Being available and accessible leads to priceless results in any business – RETENTION and LOYALTY. If you are aiming to achieve these two things, then allocate a sliver of your time in responding to e-mails, inquiries, and reacting to comments. Your customers will highly appreciate this.

Customer service thrives on the availability of the business owner. Remember that your clients may vent their dislikes via any social media platform. This means that you have a much bigger audience that will either approve or disapprove of their comments. Your engagement or the lack thereof will either make or break your social media marketing strategies.

10. **You should reciprocate.** The norm of reciprocity is essential in business. That's how social beings thrive. In order to increase your chances to succeed, you need to be able to do the same thing for others. Never expect a favor to go unreturned. This also applies to social media marketing. If you have asked other sites to link your own site to theirs, be ready to do the same. Reciprocity is vital for co-existence. And in the world of digital marketing, you will need to co-exist with millions of others.

Trust is also one of the fundamental springboards for likeability in the world of social media. If you are able to maintain trust among your digital peers, then you are more likely to gain more likes, followers, and shares.

Contrary to what most business people believe, the use of social media as a platform for marketing should not only be used by a single team in a business. Rather, the entire organization should also be involved in fostering the use of social media. These are the three important reasons why:

- The use of social media for marketing will provide opportunities for the entire organization to have an in-depth understanding of their customers;

- This will also produce a consistent voice in branding, which is vital for upholding the company's social standing in a community; and

- Social media is also an outstanding platform for real-time information dissemination

Social Media Marketing can be your ally in achieving a thriving business. If you misuse it though or create distrust within your customer base, social media can cause the downfall of you business. Take the time to learn the basics of each platform. Never cease to find ways on how you can work better and smarter using these platforms. Social media has become more powerful than ever- so it is best to strike while the digital iron is still hot! Social media is a powerful tool and you must learn to use it wisely.

Chapter 5 - Facebook Marketing

In the past, if a new business was proving to be no match against business giants, they were out of luck. Facebook has completely changed this dynamic and made it possible for even the smallest businesses to have a voice. Since Facebook marketing is favorable for both old and new business set ups, any entrepreneur can easily create his or her own marketing platform that can effectively promote their product and services.

Even if on the first try it didn't work properly, you won't have any regrets because you can always reconstruct your digital marketing plan without spending too much money. Aside from having an affordable marketing scheme, digital marketing has many media platforms to choose from, in fact it's limitless.

One of the best digital marketing platforms ever developed Facebook. Since social networking is a big deal in the virtual world, many business-marketing experts did not miss the opportunity to make it one of the ultimate mediums to market offline and online businesses.

Facebook is one of the most popular social networking sites today. Do you still remember Friendster? It's a site where the main concept captured millions of people's interest because of its personal profile creator where you could upload your personal photos and activities and you could add friends all over the world.

When Facebook emerged, its concept was somewhat similar but it had more solid applications and a greater opportunity to show anyone's personal profile. It was because of this that many saw this opportunity to try and create their business inside the network and succeed. Facebook became the goldmine of business marketing opportunities of any kind.

Benefits of Facebook Marketing

It's affordable - Once you have a Facebook account, you can create your own company page wherein you can promote your products and/or services without spending a single cent. The only thing you need to do is to exert extra effort to upload photos and videos related to your business. This way your social network audience will have the chance to become familiar with your products and/or services.

Social interaction - Through your Facebook videos and photo uploads you can easily get recognition from your potential buyers. They can easily get in touch with you if they become interested in what they find on your Facebook page. They can even comment or leave private messages on your account.

Customer support - Customer support is just within your reach because customers can directly address their concerns with you.

The big difference between Facebook marketing and other online media platforms, is that it has the biggest opportunity when it comes to business marketing, because Facebook has millions of users every day. Even a simple picture of a red ball pen can have a thousand "likes" in one day. You can start your Facebook marketing by creating your own Facebook page and first tagging your closest friends in your network. If you have 1,000 friends under your name, then don't be surprised to see your page gained close to a thousand followers. Always, check your Facebook page and post a lot of related articles, photos and music for everyone to see. Interact with your following, don't just spam post your products and expect customer loyalty.

Chapter 6 - Twitter Marketing

When the Internet craze began, a lot of social media sites came up; before, we were only using Friendster, Multiply and MySpace but as time passed, Facebook came and conquered the Internet world. However, this was just the beginning of the radical change in the World Wide Web.

Previously in Chapter 5, Facebook was introduced and I showed how it can help you advertise yourself and of course, your business to other people. I also stressed the importance of widening your social connection for different purposes. Another social network site can help your business tremendously as well – Twitter.

Much like Facebook, it is a social media network where you can interact with your friends and promote the products and services that you are offering. But what makes Twitter better than any other social media networks?

Like Facebook, Twitter is free upon registration and there are several benefits in joining the Twitter world. A lot of prominent individuals are using Twitter to share their ideas, opinions and new products (even reviews) which is relevant to ordinary people like us. We get to gain awareness from these types of things. Also, Twitter uses hash tags (#) to narrow down your searches for relevant topics. People using Twitter will tweet their thoughts and use hash tags to make sure people all over the world can access them.

Let's get to know more about the terminologies you will encounter while using Twitter.

- Tweet – it is a thought, idea, review or basically, anything a user wants to share. Tweets can be posted on the users profile or they can choose to "tweet at" somebody else. Meaning they send what they are saying to another users profile.
- Hash tag (#) – this is followed by a set or series of words you want to use to mark important words in a Tweet. Again, from what was mentioned above, Twitter users use a hash tag in a tweet so other people can easily find their tweets. For example: "I love kicking back and watching the Sunday football game #Footballfanlife #NFL." Are there rules in using a hash tag? No. You may also use several hashtag at once.
- Retweet – this means that when you are following a person and you want to share what that person posted, you can retweet it onto your own profile. This is the equivalent to a 'share' on Facebook.

- Follow- The equivalent to being someone's friend on Facebook. You will receive this persons updates. The main difference between a Facebook friendship and a follow is that you can follow someone but they do not have to follow you back and vice-versa.

So, since you are familiar with the terms used in Twitter world (twitterverse), here are the benefits you can get from using it:

- **Ultimate exposure** - Twitter is known to be one of the most trusted social networking sites. It's definitely a useful medium to market your business because everyday many people are registering on twitter, which means a lot of people in the network are potential buyers.
- **Straight forward** - Twitter also has a short and compelling word which is very useful to attract social network users. It's also easy to link on your other social network bookmarks.
- **Connection** - Because twitter is more based on interactions, once you promote your product using twitter, you'll get connected easily to your target consumer because twitter is mostly rooted in words and information, rather than pictures and videos.
- **Personal** - It's more about personal connection and ideas. If you will promote your business, you can directly talk to the people.

To start your interest with Twitter, just go to their website (www.twitter.com) and register now. All you need is your email account and there you go. Enjoy!

Chapter 7 - Instagram Marketing

In this technology based era, Instagram is one of the coolest ways to connect with your customers. According to statistics, there are almost 130 million active users on Instagram every month and everyday a whopping 1 billion photos are seen and liked. If you use this application to your advantage and the right way, then this could definitely be a big marketing success.

Setting up an Instagram account is easy as 1-2-3. All you need is a working computer or even an IOS or android phone will do, – voila! You already have an account. Here's a step-by-step guide to set up your business account:

- Create your Business Account on Instagram
- Make sure that you use your business name as your username. If already taken, then choose a username that would easily be recognized and linked to your brand
- Go ahead and complete your profile. You should definitely add an eye catching photo, a brief but informative bio and of course don't forget to add the link of your website
- Since Instagram is already owned by Facebook, you can link them to your Facebook account if you already have one. This would definitely boost and add more in your marketing strategy
- Don't forget to make a tab on your Facebook account because this would enable you to share your Instagram photos instantly to your Facebook followers.
- And finally, you can now create your Instagram content brand which focuses on the uniqueness of your brand and how you see the world. Since Instagram not only shows photos, you can also share teasing videos of your product that will capture your customer's interest.

Here are some of the advantages and reasons why Instagram is different from other social media sites:

- **Visual Marketing:** like any other social media sites, Instagram allows people to see and view your products instantly. It feeds visual stimulation that promotes interaction to your followers.
- **Levels of connection are high:** some studies show that engagement and connection with Instragram is higher than any other social media site. The amount of people liking and commenting surpasses the number of other social media sites.

- **Posts are much more noticeable:** Posts on Instagram can live on forever. They do not disappear instantly or get archived like previous tweets. On Facebook, comments or news feed updates get buried deep down the line so it usually gets lost or you will lose your interest to further go back to check it out. On Instagram, all you need to do is scroll down your profile and you will be able to highlight every post that was already posted or shared.
- **There is an emotional connection:** As the saying goes "pictures paint a thousand words" and photos shared via Instagram can easily convey emotional connection. Posting by using photos can get powerful and suggestive emotions that can produce the result that you wanted. For example, if you want to gain more donations for building a school, post a picture of kids that want to go to school but don't have the funds – then you can definitely generate a lot of donations to build your school. The power of suggestion....need I explain more?
- **Traffic Drive is much higher:** Instagram creates a higher quality of traffic. People that come from Instagram websites don't go there accidentally. They exerted an effort to click and visit your site. Because of this, they actually visit your site because they really wanted to.
- **It's fun and user friendly:** This is the best part of having an Instagram. It's simple, fast and really, really fun. Shoot your photo, write a simple description, add some hashtags and upload – you will be able to see your photos instantly. It provides you the lighter side of life and uplifts your spirit, especially seeing beautiful photos from all over the world.

How to take advantage of Instagram's features?

Here are some of the best ways you can take advantage to make your business grow and reach out to more audiences:

- *Use their new Instagram Profiles:* This gave businesses an opportunity to market on other devices aside from mobile ones. This will allow you to provide your customers a better overview of your brand and company.
- *Create contests:* Recently, there are many new photo contests being featured via Instagram. You can take advantage of this by creating your own photo contest, ask your users to participate and follow you. By this strategy, you will be able to increase your

following and at the same time. letting them get familiar with your brand.

- *Featuring your followers:* There's no better way to make your brand known than giving special treatment to your followers. This is a sure fire way of positively promoting your brand and gathering an accumulation of good reviews. Ultimately it will show photos of your followers who are genuinely happy and satisfied with your brand. This a good way of promoting yourself and your business.

Chapter 8 - Linked In Marketing

LinkedIn is among the social media platforms that are considered to be the most "professional". This is due to the fact that most of its users are key people that have expertise and specific skills in their given fields. As tagged originally, this site is crucial in finding the right candidates for positions in companies as well as for seeking out potential industries one can work for. But aside from that fact, one feature that most of us overlook is its capability to serve as an effective online tool that can actually promote our products and can help us advertise our brands in a more professional manner. LinkedIn can help us gear our branding strategy toward a newer and bolder level with the proper understanding of its salient features.

LinkedIn and its advantages

Since most of its users are key players of companies, it's no doubt that they can be your prospective clients for the products you advertise online. It has also become an avenue to look for the right people that can serve as your strategic partners in promoting your products and in getting better exposure or branding awareness.

It offers you the chance to market your products in a more professional tone. It has a built in function that enables the user to create company pages and groups that can be useful tools in brand advertising. Far more than that, it also offers you the flexibility to post, share and comment on the various contents that may trigger more site traffic.

LinkedIn is equipped with a messaging tool that helps you segment the recipients you would like to offer your products to. It gives you the power to modify your connections so that you deem them as potential clients. This also allows you to publish certain reviews or other forms of publications that may tackle the good sides of your products, thus attracting your connections to engage more with your business.

How it differs from other social media sites

It gives more than a group of people; it offers a network of professionals.

Of course, one very obvious difference to state is that this platform is mainly used for professional networking. Hence, it's most likely that you'll be dealing with professionals who in one way or another have great knowledge over a certain field. This in turn gives you the advantage to engage in different networks of professionals that help one another in achieving successful strategies in step with the online market.

It helps you establish a building tool for your online market.

Connections, akin to friends on Facebook, are your subscribers, potential clients, influencers and strategic partners that can significantly make a big difference in the fate of your online ventures. LinkedIn may actually help you find partners that can endorse your brands over a full spectrum of professional networks.

It says you're professionally backed up and that you're credible.

It has a feature that gives you the freedom to state the background and experience you have (that may actually serve as your chance to discuss the strong points of your online business). In your profile, you can actually add in some publications, certifications, and endorsements from people with relevant skills and knowledge in line with your business that can stand as proofs and testaments to how well your business really is. This in turn will give your connections the assurance that they're indeed dealing with a legitimate and credible business.

It allows you to involve all your online audiences once and for all.

The messaging feature gives you the advantage of inviting and sharing with your prospective clients the insights of your online business, and it serves as an efficient delivery system for them to be aware of the products and brands you advertise. It also has group features and company pages wherein you can open up discussions that can give clarity to questions regarding your products. This gives your connections the chance to involve themselves in the know-how operation of your business and their feedback can easily be addressed.

How to start and deal with it the right way

1. Tailor your profile by creating an account on the LinkedIn site. You can personalize your account by putting in your current career status, your academic background, your functions, as well as the other details that substantiate your identity.
2. Include in your profile the certifications you have, the trainings, the achievements and the publications and researches that may heighten your credibility.
3. Join with groups and communities that share similar interests with you and follow influences that can guide you in dealing with your business.
4. Maintain constant sharing and posting of relevant contents that advertise and promote your products to encourage more connections to check your online business.
5. Create good rapport and reputation with key professionals by involving yourself from group discussions and giving your insights regarding particular business issues online.

6. Keep updated and grow your network bigger by inviting other people and connecting with them to broaden your professional orbits and for your business to be widespread in the online world.

Chapter 9 - YouTube Marketing

In today's world, if you don't know anything about YouTube, you are missing out on a lot. Unless you are living in a rural area with no Internet connection, you have surely heard of YouTube. What you might not now is just how useful a marketing tool that YouTube can be.

Since YouTube came around, many business owners saw the great opportunity of YouTube's ability to promote any product or service. The visualization of your product being seen, potentially for free (unless you are paying YouTube to advertise for you) is like winning the grand prize lotto for business owners.

YouTube also gave many opportunities to people who own a small or medium scale commercial enterprise. You are probably aware of how much it costs to create a commercial ad these days. It costs housands and thousands of dollars for minimal ad time and very short-term contracts. YouTube has changed the advertisement game because anybody can upload a video for no charge.

How to start YouTube marketing?

Step 1: Create your own YouTube account. If you want, you can create your own YouTube channel for your products and services.

Step 2: Investigate what kind of YouTube video people are interested in.

Step 3: Watch and browse YouTube channels that you think are your possible competitors. This way you'll have an idea what kind of YouTube video you must do to attract YouTube community to watch you.

Step 4: Create the right video format (YouTube makes this very simple and they walk you through the entire process)

Step 5: Promote your video and ask common friends to share your video as a starter

How to optimize your YouTube marketing?

Step 1: Create a fascinating or compelling video, one that people can relate to.

Step 2: Make your video easy to find. Through keywords and SEO your video will become more visible

Step 3: Create a good and interesting name for your YouTube channel

Benefits of You Tube Marketing

Getting over one million viewers is certainly possible – especially since YouTube is easy to get access to globally and if you have a good, compelling video and you promote it properly, you can expect a million hits and potential buyers!

Easy to share – If people find your video beneficial and interesting they can easily get the link and share it.

Low cost –You know how much television ads cost. YouTube ads are very much affordable. And the production cost won't hurt your budget as well.

Interaction – People can easily comment about your product and services. If they're interested they will just leave you a good comment.

Video Monetization and YouTube partnership- when uploading a video chose to monetize your ads so that if lots of people view your video, YouTube will pay you. If you get enough viewers on your channel YouTube will pay you to become a partner.

Vlog- if the idea of a blog does not entice you can easily make video blogs with YouTube. These can be organized advertisements for your business or you can simply rant about whatever you want. There's no such thing as bad publicity so get your name and face out there for the world to see. People love watching videos so you should use Youtube to show the world what you and your business are all about.

Chapter 10 - Google+ Community Marketing

Another crucial social media platform that holds a promise of potential online marketing strategy for an improved content marketing practice is the Google+. Positively, Google+ is a content-driven platform that leverages your products for online branding at par with the world's best. With over 340 million (yes, million) active monthly users, Google+ is an undeniably great social media platform that you should check out!

Google+: Its positive shares of benefits

Nowadays, the power of content marketing reached the pinnacle of the online branding landscape, wherein everything can be virtually accessed in just a click. It has become very powerful that with just these online contents we read, we gain awareness of the things that are trending online and it has become very vital in a sense that they affect not only our perception of a certain product, but they eventually affect our entire purchasing decision.

Google+ offers salient features that can positively give you the advantage to propel your businesses. It is propped up with appropriate key features that may aid your business in online success.

How it differs from the rest

It is more than just the ordinary social media that you may have thought. Google+ actually helps you remain competitive in the online scene as it gives you the chance of getting a competitive edge for online marketing.

Google+ Communities Feature
Unlike other media, it gives you the flexibility in terms of online business promotions as it offers you full stretch in customizing your branding approach and allowing you to share deliverables through your "Communities". In here, you are able to network with a group of people sharing similar interests with you and you are also able to help out one another in putting up rapport that can boost your marketing skills and strategic methods.

Google+ hangouts
It's another effective mechanism that allows the user to integrate his brands to YouTube. In this feature, you can actually interact live with the people you target for your business. It gives you the freedom to discuss with them anything about your brands, thus you are candidly

establishing trust between you and your prospective clients. It has become an efficient tool as a delivery system of your products and helps you attain effective brand awareness over your business.

Explore Feature

It works similarly like the other social media sites wherein the use of the so-called "Hash tags" is evident. This very particular characteristic of Google+ enables you to employ relevant keywords that can facilitate in an easier search of your brands or products.

Google+ Circles

This attribute for the better segmentation of your prospective clients. In here, you can customize the grouping of people you target for a specific type of product. They can exclusively get the contents you share, thus attracting them to read and be more compelled of the products you advertised online.

+Post Ads Feature

This is by far the most relevant feature that can enhance you business. This feature creates a banner advertisement display that has the ability to run across searches on Google. This helps to amplify the promotion of your products to the sites that are linked up with Google features.

The ways to start and deal with it effectively

1. All you need to gear yourself up is a Google mail account. This automatically gives you the privilege to obtain your own Google+ account.
2. Once in, personalize your profile by adding exactly the items that speak to your identity and you can even tailor this by citing the features of the brands or products you want to market.
3. Claim authorship to the profile you established and now you can begin sharing content and find your target markets via circles and communities.
4. Make your Google+ posts and contents easy to find by including the Google+ Badge to your account. This will ultimately expand your reach over your prospective subscribers.
5. Once you have shared relevant content, never fail to comment and give due responses to their queries about your products. That way, you engage your subscribers in the discussion and it will help you

gain better exposure of the brand and the products you are marketing.

6. Maintain constant sharing and posting of your ads and optimize the use of its relevant features. You can even add an analytic feature to see the trends of the traffic you are marketing to.

Chapter 11 - Blog Marketing

Millions of business owners use blogs to drive traffic to their websites. Once YOU find your target customers, you can make noise through blog marketing. Business owners can make their business unique and more customized with their sense of creativity -- and that's how blog marketing works for them.

In this chapter, let's understand more about Blog Marketing. Read on to find out.

Advantages:

How is it different?

It is cost-effective

If you're a business owner, you're probably financially conscious - you want things to be better but in a more practical way. That's how blog marketing influences others, because there are a lot of platforms where you can create a blog in an affordable budget or even for free! Blog marketing just needs your creativity - you just need to have an eye for the design and your passion towards your business.

An interactive environment

People today are using search engines to find things they are interested in, so a little knowledge about SEO will surely be helpful. Once you have a blog, customers or clients can be interactive about the topics/articles on your blog by leaving a comment or suggestions. This can also be a great way to develop connections to your customers and readers.

How To Start?

Write down your target

Writing down what, or who your target audiences are before creating a blog will be very helpful as you already have an idea of what you are creating. You can write down your main goals, articles and products that you can show to your audience, it's an easy task that only needs a bit of your time and effort.

Create a blog

This is the main part of starting your blog, there's a lot of platforms that you can start with. You can choose to either buy a professional package for your blog or you can create it for next to nothing. Buy a domain name that you like, it'll be more interesting if you can come up with a domain name that is very catchy and easy to remember by your readers or customers. Once you buy a domain name (I recommend using namecheap.com), you will also need a hosting account (I recommend using hostgator.com). Once you have these two things you will be able to link your domain name to your hosting account, download Word Press for free and then start up your blog!

Wrap up

Get things done and think about what else you can add to your blog. It's all about adding that little bit of extra fun to your blog, which can bring your audience coming back for more. You can add poll questions related to your topics to boost your viewers' interactions to your site as well.

How To Do Well With It?

Be True

It's about getting the readers attraction by your original posts, accurate information, and honest opinions. A lot of people will be interested in a blogger who has good content and sense. Besides, it can help for your own credibility as a blog marketer.

Add An RSS Button

RSS button is a way for your customers/followers to follow your post through RSS readers. Just make sure that this button is placed where your customers can see it easily.

Be Active

Keep an active blog so you can monitor your followers. Also, it is a great chance to catch a potential client if you're active enough. You will able to see the sides of your marketing and study it more in the future.

So, that's how blog marketing works in a simple way, but to sum it up, it still depends on your effort if want to have a successful experience with blog marketing.

Chapter 12 - Reddit Marketing

Here's another marketing tool that most people usually forget about. It's called Reddit. Basically, Reddit is a simple community that has various links, images and it's a place where anonymity and free speech is very much welcomed. For those people who are unfamiliar with this site, Reddit is a content sharing website with a huge number of users coming from every imaginable community. Users vote on unique links, images, ideas and any other content they find worth sharing, because of this Reddit has become popular due to the rich and varied user-created content that they offer. This content ranges from animal names to the more technical and scientifically inclined discussions. The voting system allows only the best content to reach the front page of Reddit. Reddit considers itself to be the front page of the Internet, and for good reason!

Reddit is a very different online community when you compare it to the big players such as Facebook and Twitter, but it's very useful and unique, with almost thirty-four million unique visitors each month. It is so popular that the website often crashes due to high numbers of active users. Some celebrities even use it for promotions. The Daily Show has actually talked about using Reddit. They're also known for hosting the biggest Secret Santa program worldwide.

Spammers beware though, the Reddit community is known to have a strong resistance towards spam and blatant marketing attempts, however, there are still ways that you can utilize their diverse and colorful communities without being annoying and getting kicked off this valuable site.

How to Start

Research and Be Creative:

The most important part of being effective in Reddit is to fully understand how it works. Failure to do proper research often leads to an unsuccessful marketing strategy. It's also best if you read and get familiar with the Reddit etiquette, which can be found on the site itself. Do not disobey the etiquette or you will be banned in a very swift manner.

The next thing you need to do is search for subreddits by using keywords related to what you are marketing. For example, if you are selling clothes, you might find yourself in the design subreddits. Take note of the different subreddits that are relevant to your business and subscribe to all of the relevant ones.

These subreddits contain links that direct readers to external pages and each of these links has a comment section. You can sort links by popularity, by clicking the "top" button and then sorting them again by date. You need to know which links and content perform better so that we can try to create something that is similar to those. Your main goal here is to contribute and become part of a community, which has interests in the same niche that you are marketing towards. Your contribution could be as simple as giving expert insights on a discussion. This helps in creating a brand presence and will eventually help you in promoting your brand.

Make use of AskReddit:

This subreddit is a very helpful tool because it helps an individual ask direct questions and get a pool of answers from various users. It's basically a very perceptive focus group that can allow you to understand your online audience.

Try a different approach:

Try putting yourself in the shoes of a journalist. It is clear that journalists would usually use Reddit to get inspiration for their content. Popular questions would usually be picked-up by the community which, may end up getting a wider distribution, compared to having them pick-up your content directly. So, continuously posing a question that is both intriguing and interesting may be the best approach.

Reddit is an untapped resource of opportunities. Getting used to Reddit may take some time and effort, but once you get the hang of it, you'll often get far better results compared to using other social media platforms. The main thing you need to focus on is getting 'up votes' on Reddit. An up vote is the basic equivalent to a like on Facebook. If people like your post, they will up vote it and if not, they will down vote it. This system creates a sort of online democracy/ hierarchy, making Reddit one of the most trusted online sites when it comes to useful and trustworthy content.

Conclusion

Congratulations to you! I believe now that you have finished reading this book that you will have learned a lot and will now be able to utilize these social media platforms in building your own brand. Social Media Marketing is truly an influential and powerful tool once you learn to use the different platforms properly. Now that you have the knowledge of good social media marketing practices, put them to good use right away. Strategize and allow yourself to venture and create a lot of possibilities, not only personally, but for your own business venture as well. Don't waste your time now. Turn your dreams into a reality. Do not be overwhelmed by the amount of relevant social media platforms, take your time and learn them all one by one. Patience is a virtue, and this statement couldn't be truer when it comes to business.

It was an honor and pleasure writing this book and sharing it with keen online marketers like you. It gave me a sense of accomplishment knowing that I was able to help others understand and give a clearer picture on how social media marketing works. Always remember that you can refer back to this book anytime you need it.

Again, thanks for purchasing this book. Be sure to share your experience and if you enjoyed this book, please take the time to share your thoughts and post a review on Amazon. It'd be greatly appreciated!

Good luck and may you have a prosperous business! Create your own, unique brand and begin to thrive today!